TRACKING DOWN

MEDIEVAL LIFE

IN BRITAIN

TRACKING DOWN

MEDIEVAL LIFE

IN BRITAIN

MOIRA BUTTERFIELD

W
FRANKLIN WATTS
LONDON · SYDNEY

First published in 2010 by Franklin Watts

Copyright © 2010 Franklin Watts

Franklin Watts
338 Euston Road
London NW1 3BH

Franklin Watts Australia
Level 17/207 Kent Street
Sydney, NSW 2000

A CIP catalogue record for this book is available
from the British Library.

Dewey number: 941'.03

ISBN 978 0 7496 9235 3

Printed in China

Franklin Watts is a division of Hachette Children's Books,
an Hachette UK company.

www.hachette.co.uk

Editor: Sarah Ridley
Design: John Christopher/White Design
Editor in Chief: John C. Miles
Art director: Jonathan Hair
Picture research: Diana Morris

Picture credits: © The Board of Trustees of the Armouries: 12r. Ashmolean Museum Oxford/Bridgeman
Art Library: 17t. Keith Brewster Photography: 24. British Library London/Art Archive: 7, 9tr, 10.
British Library/HIP/Topfoto: 9bl, 17b. The Company of Merchant Adventurers of the City of York: 19bl.
The Granger Collection/Topfoto: 8. Hoberman Collection UK/Alamy: 29tr. Neil Holden/PD: 19tr.
Angelo Hornak/Corbis: 22, 23bl, 29bl, 30. Michael Jones/Alamy: 28. Nadia Mackenzie/National Trust:
14t, 15t. Manu/Alamy: front cover, 13. Musée Condé Chantilly/Gianni Dagli Orti/Art Archive: 23tr.
Museum of London: 11t, 11b, 27c. Norton Priory Museum Trust: 20, 21tr on loan from National
Museums Liverpool (WAG 6233). Chris Parker/Corbis: 14b. Picturepoint/Topham: 26b.
David Ross/www.britainexpress.com: 15c. John Shaw/Eye Ubiquitous/Alamy: 21bl. Topfoto: 12t. Victoria
& Albert Museum London/AAA Collection: 25bl. Victoria & Albert Museum London/Sally Chappel/Art
Archive: 25tr. Collection Jean Vigne/Archives Nationale Paris/Kharbine-Tapabor/Art Archive: 27tr. Patrick
Ward/Corbis: 18. Weald and Downland Open Air Museum: 16. Andy Williams/Loop Images/Corbis: 6.
*Every attempt has been made to clear copyright. Should there be any inadvertent omission please apply to
the publisher for rectification.*

CONTENTS

MEDIEVAL BRITAIN

Historians give names to different periods of time in British history. The years between 1066 and 1485 are called 'the medieval age' or 'the middle ages'. It was the era when castles and cathedrals appeared around Britain, and knights fought on horseback.

➜ The village of Welford-on-Avon still has many medieval houses and a church built in medieval times.

Medieval life

Most ordinary people lived in small villages and farmed patches of land to grow food for their families. They spent their time working in the fields or looking after their animals. Then gradually, over time, more and more people began to live in towns and cities, working as merchants or craftspeople. Britain had become a busier, more prosperous kingdom by the end of the age.

Fighting for the throne

Medieval kings were all-powerful. Everybody owed them allegiance (loyalty), and they made the laws and collected taxes (money) from their people to use however they wished. During this period in history there were often wars between different nobles claiming the English crown. Kings were sometimes overthrown and even murdered. Wales and part of France belonged to the medieval English kingdom, but Scotland and Ireland had their own rulers.

➜ King Edward I (reigned from 1272 to 1307) sits on his throne. Churchmen and nobles stand in front of him.

LOOK FOR

Medieval buildings

Medieval buildings still survive around the country. Look out for them in market towns and villages, and in the oldest parts of cities. Medieval Britain was a lot less crowded than it is today. The population (number of people) in Britain was about 5 million in 1350. That compares to roughly 59 million people today.

Churches everywhere

Medieval life was difficult and short, but people believed they would have a better life in heaven after they died. The Catholic Church was the religion of the land, and everyone went to their local church regularly. Lots of small stone churches were built around the country, as well as some large cathedrals, which powerful and important churchmen used as their base. Their high towers could be seen by everyone for miles around, and were a symbol of Church power.

MEDIEVAL PEOPLE

Medieval Britain was run as a 'feudal system', which meant there were strict rules about who people obeyed and who owned the land. Everybody had a set position in society, with the king at the top and the peasants at the bottom.

King in charge

The king owned all the land in his kingdom. Below him were the Lords, his most important nobles. The king granted them big estates – large areas of land – in return for service. This meant providing men to fight for the king when he needed them. When they died, nobles handed on their titles and land to their children, but if a noble fell out with his king he was likely to have everything taken away. The king also granted lands to the Church.

♠ Life at the top: this medieval manuscript painting shows the coronation of King Edward III in 1327.

LOOK FOR

Medieval treasures

Your local museum may have some of these typical medieval finds:

Rubbish Lots of ordinary objects from medieval times have been found, often in sites that were once used as rubbish tips.

Writing Hand-written books, letters and records have survived, and towards the end of the era books were printed for the first time.

Knights are next

Below the nobles were the knights, who had the title 'Sir' in front of their name. Each noble had his own group of loyal knights, and he granted each one a manor and land to go with it. In return, a knight had to fight for his Lord a certain number of days a year. The knight swore 'fealty' (loyalty) to his Lord and was his 'vassal' (sworn servant). Towards the end of the medieval age, the role of knight began to change. Some became full-time professional soldiers with a wage, and others paid a fee not to fight at all.

◄ Knights were supposed to be chivalrous: brave, honourable and always ready to fight for their ladies.

Peasants come last

Knights rented out their land to tenants, mostly peasants who lived by farming and paid their rent to the knight by giving him money and crops. A knight would employ servants to help him run his lands and collect rent from the peasants. His officials also checked up on any local shops and flour mills he owned, to make sure they were being run well by his tenants. A knight had a duty to look after his estate, and if he ran it badly his tenants might start complaining about him to his Lord.

▲ A peasant cares for sheep in a pen.
A peasant's daily work began at dawn.

In 1066 William of Normandy invaded and took the kingdom from King Harold, who was killed at the Battle of Hastings. William began to build castles to defend his power, and the most famous is the White Tower, now part of the Tower of London.

A new kind of castle

The White Tower was a massive square stone building called a keep, surrounded by walls and ditches. Before this time, English leaders lived mainly in wooden buildings, and few people in England had seen such a castle before. It sent out a powerful message about who was now in charge.

➜ The White Tower in London, surrounded by walls. It was ideal as a prison, a treasure store and a place for the king to hide in times of trouble.

Death in the Tower

Over time the White Tower became one of the largest and strongest fortresses in the land. It is connected with medieval stories of murder and execution, including the mysterious disappearance of thirteen-year-old Edward V and his younger brother in 1483. It's thought they were killed and buried in the White Tower, possibly on the orders of their uncle, who took the throne and became Richard III.

GO VISIT

The Tower of London and the Museum of London

At the Tower of London you can visit rooms in the White Tower where kings once slept. There is even a reconstruction of a royal bed used by medieval monarch Edward I. You can see weapons of the time and find out about some of the exciting and scary stories connected to the Tower. Across the city all sorts of everyday objects from medieval London are on show at the Museum of London, including brooches, buckles, shoes, jugs, coins and books.

⬇ This ring-shaped silver brooch is part of the collection in the Museum of London (see below).

Who had what

In 1085 William the Conquerer ordered a survey of his new kingdom, and sent teams of servants around England to record what property people owned. The record they made is called the Domesday Book, and it tells us a lot about English life in William's time. It lists over 13,000 settlements, and records what buildings there were, how many people lived there, and even how many farm animals they owned. The Domesday manuscripts are now in The National Archives at Kew, London.

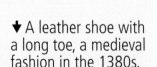

⬇ A leather shoe with a long toe, a medieval fashion in the 1380s.

LAND OF CASTLES

Medieval monarchs and nobles built castle strongholds across Britain. Lots of them still exist, including Harlech Castle in Wales.

Powerful place

Harlech was one of several castles that Edward I built to stop the Welsh rebelling against his rule in the late 1200s. It had stone walls, towers and a big gatehouse. The narrow entrance was fitted with portcullises (heavy iron grilles that could be raised or lowered), and some 'murder holes' in the roof. Troops defending the castle could fire arrows down through these holes or pour something harmful, such as boiling water or oil, onto any attackers below.

◀ Harlech Castle was built with high walls, towers and one narrow entrance, so it was very hard to attack.

GO VISIT
Castles and weapon displays

At Harlech Castle you can see a heap of stone cannonballs left over from a medieval siege. At Caerphilly Castle, also in Wales, you can see reproductions of medieval 'siege engines', including giant catapults used to fire missiles such as stones at castle walls. At the Royal Armouries in Leeds you can see medieval weapons and armour, including swords, helmets and even a 'shaffron' – a helmet made for a warhorse.

➜ A medieval knight's sword was a heavy weapon. This 14th-century example was found during an excavation.

Life inside

Inside the castle there was a Great Hall and a private suite called the 'solar' for the Lord and his family. There would also have been workshops, a bakery, kitchens and a chapel, and it would have been a busy place full of scurrying servants and guards. It would have been cold and smelly, though, heated only by smoky fires and with no toilets other than holes in the wall that led down to trenches outside.

Scene of sieges

The only way to conquer a castle was to besiege it – surround it and smash the walls down or starve the people inside into surrender. To damage walls, attackers used siege engines – big wooden catapults or battering rams. Another way to take a castle was to dig a tunnel underneath the walls so that they would collapse. King John's army did this to some rebellious nobles at Rochester Castle in Kent, in 1215.

➜ The keep of Rochester Castle today. Although one tower collapsed when a mine was dug under it in 1215, the rebels resisted until food supplies ran out.

Knights were less important than Lords and lived, not in grand castles, but in country houses called manors. Ightham Mote, in Kent, is an example of a medieval manor that still survives today. It was first built in the 1300s.

Smoky inside

The knight would entertain in the Great Hall, and some of his family and servants would sleep there, probably on sacks stuffed with straw. He and his wife would live in the more luxurious solar rooms, where they would have a bed, tapestries on the walls and a bowl for washing. The manor was heated by wood fires and the smoke would have drifted around and up through the roof.

↑ The Great Hall at Ightham Mote.

↓ Ightham had a moat, probably to defend it from robbers rather than armies.

You can visit Ightham Mote and see the medieval tomb of Sir Thomas Cawne, one of Ightham Mote's first owners, in the church nearby. His life-size stone effigy (image) is shown wearing battle armour from the 1300s. He probably fought at the Battle of Crécy in 1346, alongside the Black Prince, son of King Edward III (find out about the prince's tomb on page 23). At Ightham Mote you can see a sculpture depicting the Black Prince on horseback.

⬇ The effigy of Sir Thomas Cawne shows him in medieval armour. He fought with the Black Prince, shown above.

Life at the manor

The knight rented out the buildings and land in the village nearby, and his managers would go round checking up on his property and collecting rent for him. When he wasn't overseeing his estate he would go out hunting with trained dogs and hawks, or perhaps watch his squires do some fighting practice. Each knight would be in charge of one or two young squires, the sons of other knights. He was expected to train them up to one day become knights themselves.

Lady in charge

Knights sometimes had to leave their homes for long periods of time, to fight for their Lord. When a knight was away, his wife had to run his estate and defend it from enemies. She had the help of his managers – a steward to manage the manor and a reeve to collect taxes from the villagers. Her day would include overseeing the servants, praying in the chapel and spending the evening in the solar. She might do some needlework, spin wool and play music and games such as chess.

A PEASANT'S HOME

Most ordinary medieval people lived in small country villages. Their simple homes have long since disappeared, but archaeologists have worked out what they might have looked like. A typical peasant's cottage has been rebuilt at the Weald and Downland Open Air Museum in Sussex.

➜ All kinds of historical buildings have been rescued and rebuilt at the Weald and Downland Open Air Museum.

Crowded and dark

The peasant's cottage at the Weald and Downland Open Air Museum has two rooms, a main one with an open fireplace and a smaller one with a simple oven in it. A family of four or five people would have shared the rooms, sleeping wherever they could find space, on sacks filled with straw, and using a pit dug outside as a toilet. They ate very simple food that they grew themselves, mostly a kind of vegetable and grain stew called pottage, with lumps of meat added on special occasions.

The Weald and Downland Open Air Museum and the Ashmolean Museum

The museum in Sussex has medieval shops and houses furnished the way they would have been centuries ago. Pottery was found in most homes, and pieces often turn up around villages and towns. The Ashmolean Museum in Oxford has a big pottery collection, some marked with the original fingerprints of their medieval makers.

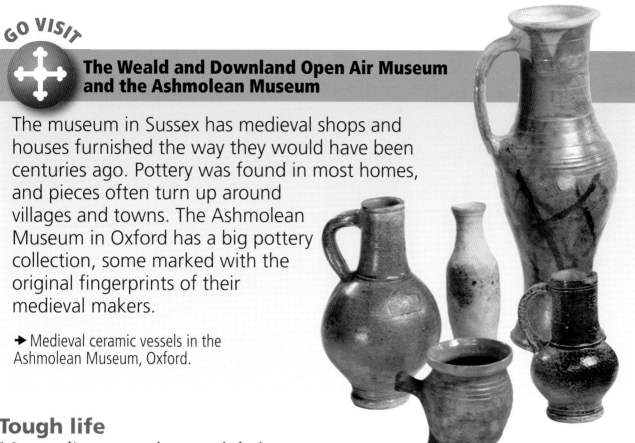

→ Medieval ceramic vessels in the Ashmolean Museum, Oxford.

Tough life

Most ordinary people never left the area where they were born. They would spend their days working the land they rented from the local knight, occasionally working for him on his land, too. Life was tough, especially if the weather was bad and the crops failed. Then families starved, and if a peasant could not pay his rent, he might be thrown off his land for good.

▼ Peasants at work – a picture from the *Luttrell Psalter*, a 14th-century manuscript.

The mystery of Hangleton

The peasant's cottage at the Weald and Downland Open Air museum is based on remains found at Hangleton in Sussex. It was once a busy village but it was abandoned by the end of the 1300s, probably due to famine (starvation) and the Black Death; a terrible disease that arrived in England in 1348. It killed a third of all the people in Europe.

BUSINESS MEDIEVAL STYLE

Towns began to grow bigger in medieval times. They were centres of business and government, just as towns and cities are today. In York you can still visit a medieval business headquarters, called the Merchant Adventurers' Hall.

Getting together

Medieval craftsmen and businessmen organised themselves together in groups called guilds. The Merchant Adventurers were a group of York mercers (traders) who sold cargoes in other parts of the world and brought back goods to sell at home. They sent their ships from the river port of York to northern countries such as Iceland and Russia, taking British exports such as wool and bringing back imports such as sealskins and fur. It was a profitable but risky business. If a trader's ship sank he could lose all his money.

▼ Inside the Merchant Adventurers' Hall, where local businessmen met to discuss their work.

Deals, prayers and cures

Members of the Merchant Adventurers used their wealth to build a hall between 1357 and 1361, as a place for them to have meetings and do business. Religion was important to them, too, and part of the building was set aside as a chapel for worship. In the undercroft (the cellars), they also set up a charitable hospital to help local people. A number of medieval guilds still survive today, including the Merchant Adventurers, who still run their hall and organise charity work.

GO VISIT

Merchant Adventurers' Hall, York

In the Merchant Adventurers' Hall you can see a long wooden chest, called the 'evidence chest', made in the 1300s to store important documents. Medieval people often had a heavy carved chest where they kept their most important possessions. In 1483 Richard III visited York and the guilds of the town met him, carrying banners that represented their trades. The banners have been remade and now hang in the Adventurers' Hall.

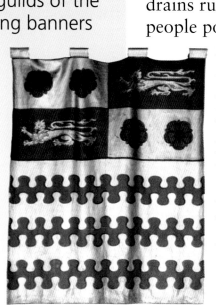

➔ The impressive heraldic banner of the Merchant Adventurers.

DIEV·NOVS·DONNE·BONNE·ADVENTVRE

Merchants hall

⬆ The coat-of-arms – the official badge – of the Merchant Adventurers. The motto is Latin for: 'God give us good fortune'.

Smelly streets

Medieval towns were usually surrounded by defensive walls, with large easily-defended gateways for getting in and out. They had higgledy-piggledy narrow streets with open drains running along them, where people poured their waste water. Some residents would have kept animals that roamed freely, and vermin such as rats would have thrived in the smelly rubbish-strewn alleyways. Houses were built from wood and plaster, or stone if they were for wealthier people. There were shops, craft workshops, taverns and usually a busy marketplace.

Many men and women devoted their lives to prayer by becoming monks or nuns. Men lived in priories (also called monasteries) and women lived in convents (also called nunneries). The remains of a typical priory are preserved at Norton Priory in Cheshire, but you can find examples all over Britain.

➜ The undercroft of Norton Priory, built in the late 12th century.

Inside a priory

Norton Priory was home to about 25 religious men. Unusually for a priory, they weren't monks, but a kind of priest called a canon, with an abbot in charge. Their home had a church and lots of other buildings such as kitchens, a dormitory to sleep in and a big cellar area called an undercroft, for storing food and drink. There were rooms for pilgrims – travellers who visited the priory to see its religious treasures – and a herb garden for growing medicinal plants. In some monasteries there was also a scriptorium, where monks copied religious manuscripts by hand and decorated them with beautiful pictures called 'illumination'.

Ruled by the bell

Every day a bell was rung to mark several different prayer times that monks or canons had to attend, beginning with Matins at about 2am in the morning and ending with Compline in the evening. The monks ate twice a day in silence while listening to religious readings in Latin. We know from remains found at Norton Priory that the people who lived there ate simple meals of meat, bread and vegetables and drank lots of weak beer which they brewed themselves.

➤ The statue of Saint Christopher, thought to bring good luck and protection to travellers who touched it.

GO VISIT

Norton Priory

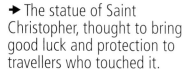

Norton Priory had two religious relics that pilgrims came to see. One was supposedly a piece of the true cross on which Jesus was crucified. The other was a statue of Saint Christopher (left), the patron saint of travellers, who was thought to protect pilgrims on their journeys. The statue is still on display. It would have been brightly painted in medieval times.

A religious business

Priories were run as businesses. They owned farmland and buildings for miles around, mostly rented out to farmers and tradesmen. They also made an income from visiting pilgrims and usually had rich patrons – local nobles who donated money. Some monks would be 'lay brothers', which meant they attended to the business of running their priory – perhaps by working on the priory's own farm, in the garden or in the kitchens. Others would be 'choir monks', who spent their time singing and praying.

◄ Tombs in the ruins of Norton Priory. Rich people were buried in the Priory church, as near to the altar as possible.

BUILT FOR GOD

Spectacular cathedrals were built in towns across Britain, soaring skyward to glorify God and remind everyone who saw them how important the Church was. Canterbury Cathedral in Kent was particularly famous because it was an important place of pilgrimage and was also home to the head of the English Church, the Archbishop of Canterbury.

Church centre

The stone cathedral was first built in the 1070's by the Normans (see page 10), on the site of an older church. It was designed to impress, with decorated ceilings, spectacular archways, stained-glass windows and a large monastery attached to it. A church is called a cathedral if it houses a cathedra – the throne of a bishop – and a very high-ranking churchman, the Archbishop of Canterbury, was in charge of the new church. Senior churchmen were as powerful as nobles in medieval times, and could advise and even criticise kings. The ultimate leader of the Church was the Pope, based in Rome, who was as powerful as a monarch.

← The aisle at Canterbury Cathedral, designed to impress visitors with the power of the Church and the glory of God.

Murder in the cathedral

In 1170 Thomas Becket, the Archbishop of Canterbury, was murdered in Canterbury Cathedral, apparently on the orders of King Henry II. Becket had argued with the King about royal policy towards the Church, and was killed by sword blows from four of the King's knights. The murder shocked the country and Becket was proclaimed a martyr (a holy saint). The guilt-ridden King walked barefoot to Becket's tomb to pray for forgiveness, and it soon became a shrine attracting thousands of pilgrims every year.

↑ A 15th-century manuscript painting showing the murder of Thomas Becket.

GO VISIT

Canterbury Cathedral

At the cathedral you can see a shrine set up on the spot where Becket was murdered. You can also see the tomb of the Black Prince, the son of Edward III. He was a famous medieval warrior who fought battles for his father. His bronze likeness is dressed in armour.

➡ The Black Prince's armour is carved with royal leopards.

A holy holiday

A pilgrimage to Canterbury Cathedral was a kind of medieval holiday. Travellers stayed at inns and priories on the journey, which could take weeks. They believed that by praying at the shrine of Thomas Becket they would be forgiven for past sins, and would stand more chance of getting into heaven. A famous medieval book, *The Canterbury Tales*, by Geoffrey Chaucer, follows a group of pilgrims on their way to Canterbury.

Most ordinary medieval people would only see art when they went to church and saw wall paintings that told stories from the Bible. A few have survived, including a fine example at the Church of St Peter and Paul at Chaldon, Surrey.

➤ The paintings at Chaldon Church were hidden under plaster for centuries, and rediscovered in Victorian times.

Behave, or else

The paintings are a dire warning of what would happen to sinners. The archangel Michael weighs up the good and bad deeds that people have done in their earthly life, and the good ones climb up the ladder of souls to heaven above. The bad ones tumble down the ladder to hell, where devils wait for them. The artist depicts sinful people being tortured by devils who nibble their feet, poke them with forks or shove them into fires. One example shows a drunken pilgrim who has sold his cloak to buy wine. Another shows a miser being roasted as he is forced to count the money that pours out of his mouth.

Mystery artists

No-one knows who painted the pictures at Chaldon, or at other churches around the country. The artists may have been travelling monks because they seemed to know the Bible stories well. They used paint made from natural minerals ground up into different-coloured powder and mixed with whitewash or black charcoal to make lighter or darker shades. The artists added egg yolk, buttermilk or linseed oil to make the paint thick. Occasionally they used expensive colours brought from abroad – blue made from a gemstone called lapis lazuli and red made from a kind of mineral called cinnibar.

GO VISIT

Victoria and Albert Museum

The Victoria and Albert Museum in London has lots of beautiful medieval treasures that show the skill of the craftsmen of the time. This Gloucester Candlestick is made of precious metal and intricately carved with humans, monkeys and dragons. The Devonshire Hunting Tapestries (see below) are also at the museum.

Art for the wealthy

Rich people had art hanging on their walls in the form of tapestries, handmade by skilled craftspeople. They often showed hunting scenes, such as the boar and bear-hunting on these Devonshire Hunting Tapestries, once owned by an English noble. The huntsmen are shown in a beautiful flower-filled landscape, along with fashionably-dressed courtiers.

← A part of the Devonshire Tapestries, showing bears being hunted by huntsmen on horseback.

GOING TO SCHOOL

The first schools and universities in Britain were founded in medieval times. Some were based in priories or cathedrals. Others were founded with grants from merchants or rich nobles. One of the oldest schools still in use today is Winchester College in Hampshire. The first scholars (schoolboys) arrived there in 1394.

The first schools

The children of nobles were educated at home, but the bright male children of merchants or wealthy farmers went to new schools such as Winchester. It was founded by a bishop, and some of the scholars were quiristers, which meant they were choristers who sang in the school chapel when they weren't at their lessons. Schoolboys of the time would have lived at their school from about the age of seven, and had their hair cut in a tonsure – short with a shaved patch on the top, like a monk.

▼A courtyard at Winchester College, where medieval schoolboys would have once walked.

A medieval lesson

Young scholars started by learning the alphabet and the Ten Commandments from the Bible. Later they learnt to write and translate Latin, the main written language of medieval Europe. They would scratch notes on tablets covered in wax, or they might be given ink, pen and parchment. Later on in medieval times paper and printed books became more common. Teachers were usually churchmen, and they carried a birch, a tied-up bundle of twigs used to hit boys who misbehaved or did not learn fast enough.

→ These medieval manuscript paintings show scholars at work and praying to the Virgin Mary.

GO VISIT

Writing treasures

At the Museum of London you can see medieval writing tablets that would have been filled with wax. Notes could be made using a little tool called a stylus. The museum also has a rare page (right) from a 1476 printed edition of Chaucer's *Canterbury Tales,* (see page 23). This was one of the first books ever printed in England. Earlier editions of the book were copied by hand.

Off to college

The earliest British university was Oxford, which began in the 11th century. There were fights between the students and the townspeople of Oxford, so when Henry VI founded King's College, Cambridge, in 1441, he set strict rules to make sure the students behaved. They weren't allowed to wear brightly-coloured stockings, pointed shoes, stripey hoods, long hair or beards and they couldn't keep animals in their rooms!

CROWNED AND BURIED

English kings were crowned and also buried at Westminster Abbey in London. The medieval era was a violent time for nobles. A number of kings were killed in battle, along with their aristocratic supporters. At times civil war raged across the land.

The latest style

The Abbey we can see today was begun in 1245, and was built in what was then the latest style, called Gothic. The church has a long nave running up to an altar, with chapels built on either side. The stonemasons added Gothic features – pointed arches, ribbed vaulting (stone ceiling supports curved like rib-bones), rose windows (giant round stained-glass windows) and flying buttresses (big outside supports that arch outwards). These designs were used in lots of medieval cathedrals around Europe.

⬇ The front of Westminster Abbey.

GO VISIT

Westminster Abbey, London

Westminster Abbey is a treasurehouse of medieval tombs and architecture. Lots of medieval tombs are to be found in its chapels, many of them with carved images of monarchs and their relatives. In the museum attached to the church you can see more medieval treasures, such as the sword, helmet and shield of Henry V, carried at his funeral in 1422.

➡ An effigy (carved image) on the tomb of Henry III, King of England from 1216-1272. He was crowned at the age of nine.

Crowning chair

Westminster Abbey is the home of the Coronation Chair, an oak throne that English sovereigns sit on when they are crowned. It was made in 1296 for King Edward I. He fought against the Scots, who had their own medieval monarchs, and he captured the Stone of Scone – the stone on which Scottish kings were crowned. He had the chair designed with a space underneath to hold the Stone, but it was given back to Scotland in 1996.

➜ The Coronation Chair, with an empty compartment underneath where the Stone of Scone once rested.

The end of the medieval era

During the 1400s there was civil war in England between the two noble families of York and Lancaster, who both claimed the crown. The struggle is called the Wars of the Roses because both families had rose emblems. They fought a number of battles across England, and nobles on both sides were imprisoned and executed. The wars ended in victory for the Lancastrians in 1485. Yorkist Richard III was killed and Henry Tudor took the crown and became Henry VII, founding the Tudor dynasty of kings and queens. Henry is buried in Westminster Abbey.

GLOSSARY

Archbishop The highest ranking churchman in the English Church.

Bishop A high-ranking churchman in charge of the priests and churches in a particular area.

Black Death A deadly plague that killed millions of people across Europe in the 1340s.

Domesday Book A set of handwritten records of 13,000 medieval English settlements, listing the buildings, the number of people and details such as the animals they owned.

Effigy A life-sized carved image of someone, found on medieval tombs.

Fealty An oath of allegiance made by a medieval man to someone ranking above him in society.

Feudal system A system whereby the monarch and important nobles rented out land to lesser nobles in return for military service. Lesser nobles rented out land to farmers and tradesmen in return for work, rent and a share of crops.

Gothic A medieval style of architecture used to build cathedrals.

Guild An officially organised group of medieval businessmen or craftsmen.

Illumination Hand-painted colourful decorations around an individual letter or a manuscript.

Keep The square-shaped stronghold in the centre of a castle.

Knight A lesser noble with the title of 'Sir', who has taken an oath of allegiance to a higher-ranking noble and may be called on to fight for his Lord.

Lord An important noble and powerful landowner, next down in importance from the king.

Manor The country house of a knight, with ownership of the land and villages around it.

Pilgrimage A long journey made to a religious site, to pray.

Portcullis A heavy iron grille that could be pulled up or dropped down to act as a castle gate.

Pottage A grain and vegetable stew eaten by medieval peasants.

Priory A religious community of monks led by a prior.

Reeve A tax-collector who worked for a knight, collecting rent from his tenants.

Relic Sacred remains, such as body parts of a religious saint or pieces of the cross on which Jesus was crucified.

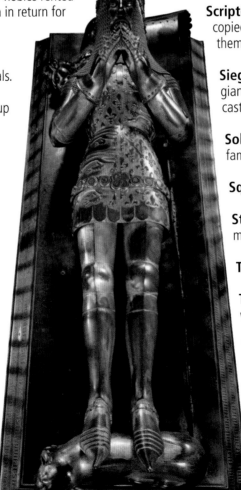

Scriptorium A special room where monks copied out religious manuscripts and decorated them with coloured pictures.

Siege engines Wooden battering rams and giant catapults designed to fire stones at castle walls.

Solar Private room for a noble and his family.

Squire A young trainee-knight.

Steward An official who helped to manage a knight's estate.

Tapestry A woven hanging for a wall.

Tudor The family name of the monarchs who ruled after the medieval age.

Vassal Sworn servant. Lords were vassals of the King. Knights were vassals of their Lords.

PLACES TO VISIT

Ashmolean Museum
Beaumont Street
Oxford
OX1 2PH
www.ashmolean.org/collections/

Caerphilly Castle
Caerphilly
Cardiff
CF83 1JD
www.cadw.wales.gov.uk

Canterbury Cathedral
The Precincts
Canterbury
CT1 2EH
www.canterbury-cathedral.org

Harlech Castle
Harlech
Gwynedd
LL46 2YH
www.castlewales.com/harlech

Ightham Mote
Mote Road
Ivy Hatch
Sevenoaks
Kent
TN15 0NT
www.nationaltrust.org.uk

Merchant Adventurers' Hall
Fossgate
York
YO1 9XD
www.theyorkcompany.co.uk

Museum of London
150 London Wall
London
EC2Y 5HN
www.museumoflondon.org.uk

Norton Priory
Tudor Road
Manor Park
Runcorn
Cheshire
WA7 1SX
www.nortonpriory.org

Rochester Castle
Rochester
Kent
ME1 1SW
www.english-heritage.org.uk

Royal Armouries Leeds
Armouries Drive
Leeds
LS10 1LT
www.royalarmouries.org/leeds

Tower of London
The Tower of London
London
EC3N 4AB
www.hrp.org.uk/TowerOfLondon

Victoria and Albert Museum
Cromwell Road
London
SW7 2RL
www.vam.ac.uk

Weald and Downland Museum
Singleton
Chichester
West Sussex
PO18 0EU
www.wealddown.co.uk

Westminster Abbey
20 Dean's Yard
London
SW1P 3PA
www.westminster-abbey.org

WEBLINKS
Here are some websites with information about medieval life in Britain, and some of the sites in this book.
www.britishmuseum.org
Go to the 'explore' section and browse through over 4,000 objects in the museum collection. There is also an 'explore' section specifically on medieval Europe.
www.bbc.co.uk/history/british/middle_ages
Lots of information, and a Wars of the Roses battlefield game to try.
www.nationaltrust.org.uk
Search for medieval buildings looked after by the National Trust.

Note to parents and teachers
Every effort has been made by the Publishers to ensure that the websites in this book are suitable for children, that they are of the highest educational value, and that they contain no inappropriate or offensive material. However, because of the nature of the Internet, it is impossible to guarantee that the contents of these sites will not be altered. We strongly advise that Internet access is supervised by a responsible adult.

INDEX

art 24-25
Ashmolean Museum 17

Battle of Hastings 10
Becket, Thomas 23
Black Death 17, 30
Black Prince 15, 23
books 8, 11, 27

Caerphilly Castle 12
Canterbury Cathedral 22, 23
Canterbury Tales, The 23, 27
castles 6, 10-11, 12-13, 14, 30
cathedrals 6, 7, 22, 23, 26, 28, 30
Cawne, Sir Thomas 15
Chaucer, Geoffrey 23, 27
Church 7, 8, 20-23, 22, 23, 30
churches 6, 7, 15, 20, 21, 22, 24, 28, 30
Coronation Chair 29
craftsmen 6, 18, 19, 25, 30

Devonshire Hunting Tapestries 25
Domesday Book 11, 30

education 26-27

farming 6, 9, 11, 16, 17, 21, 30
fealty 9, 30
feudal system 8-9, 30
food 6, 13, 16, 20, 21

Gloucester Candlestick 25
Great Hall 13, 14
guilds 18, 19, 30

Harlech Castle 12, 13
houses 6, 14-17, 19

Ightham Mote 14-15

King Edward I 7, 11, 12, 29
King Edward III 8, 15, 23
King Edward V 11, 28
King Harold 10
King Henry II 23
King Henry III 28
King Henry VI 27
King Henry VII 29
King Richard III 11, 19, 29
knights 6, 9, 12, 14-15, 17, 23, 30

Lords 8, 9, 13, 14, 15, 30

manors 9, 14-15, 30
Merchant Adventurers' Hall 16, 17
merchants (mercers) 6, 16, 17, 26
monasteries 20, 21, 22
monks 20, 21, 25, 26, 30
Museum of London 11, 27

nobles 7, 8, 9, 12-13, 21, 22, 25, 26, 28, 29, 30
Norton Priory 20-21
nuns 20

peasants 8, 9, 16-17, 30
pilgrimages 21, 22, 23, 30
pilgrims 20, 21, 23, 24
priories 20-21, 23, 26, 30

reeves 15, 30
religion 7, 19, 20-23, 24, 25
Rochester Castle 13, 31
Royal Armouries 12

St Peter and St Paul Church, Chaldon 24-25
school 26, 27
scriptoriums 20, 21, 30
sieges 12, 13
solar 13, 14, 15, 30
squires 15, 30
stewards 15, 30
Stone of Scone 29

tombs 15, 21, 23, 28, 29, 30
Tower of London 10, 11
towns 6, 7, 17, 18, 19, 22

universities 26, 27

Victoria and Albert Museum 25
villages 6, 7, 15, 16-17, 30

Wales 7, 12
wall paintings 24
Wars of the Roses 29
Weald and Downland Open Air Museum 16, 17
weapons 11, 12, 13, 28
Westminster Abbey 28-29
White Tower 10, 11
William the Conqueror/of Normandy 10-11
Winchester College 26

Here are the lists of contents for each title in *Tracking Down...*

World War II in Britain

What was World War II? • Running the war • Defending Britain
The battles in the sky • Early warning systems • Air-raid shelters
Life on the Home Front • The children's war • Women in action
The war at sea • The Normandy landings • The end of the war

The Romans in Britain

Romans in Britain • People in Roman Britain • An army base
Busy Londinium • Britain gets roads • Soldier's town • Hadrian's wall
Roman baths and temples • See the show • A country villa
A mystery palace • Enemies from the sea

The Anglo-Saxons in Britain

All about the Anglo-Saxons • Anglo-Saxon people
Last stand of the Brits • Tomb of a king • An ancient church •
Warriors rule • A monk who made history • A Saxon village
A king in hiding • A king's city • One true king • The last battle

The Victorians in Britain

Who were the Victorians? • Queen Victoria at home • Running the country
Industry and manufacturing • The railway age • New ideas and engineering
Beside the seaside • Everyday life • Grand homes for the rich
Children and schools • Victorian health • Crime and punishment

The Vikings in Britain

All about the Vikings • Viking people • Lindisfarne • A great army
A Viking farm • A Viking town • Viking laws • Viking treasure
Shipped to heaven • Viking runes and art • Terror returns • Here to stay

Medieval Life in Britain

All about Medieval Times • Medieval people • The White Tower
Harlech Castle • A manor house • Life as a peasant • Adventurers' Hall
Inside a priory • A cathedral • Medieval art
Going to school • Westminster Abbey

Tudors and Stuarts in Britain

All about Tudor and Stuart Britain • Tudor and Stuart people
Hampton Court palace • Reformation ruins • A dangerous tower
Disaster at sea • A grand house • A trip to the theatre
A busy kitchen • Civil war • A living manor • A monarch's cathedral